MW01713994

@Supermarket:

Package Designs

スーパーマーケットデザイン［食品・飲料・日用品のパッケージ］

Photo by Waitrose

Contents

はじめに

海外に行ったら、必ず立ち寄りたいのがスーパーマーケットである。乳製品のイラストやお菓子のパッケージなど、その国に昔からあるものや、最近の流行など、暮らしに根付いたデザインが揃っている。

スーパーマーケットという場所の利点は、どこに行っても同じクオリティの商品が手に入ることだった。しかし同じ商品に満足した消費者たちは、どこにもない選ばれた商品や、そこでしか買えないオリジナリティのある商品を揃える、個性のあるスーパーに魅力を感じ始めている。

どこのスーパーマーケットを選ぶかで、その人のライフスタイルがわかると言われるイギリスや、オーガニック専門のスーパーが人気を集めるBIOブームのサンフランシスコ。オリジナル商品のデザインに力を入れるオランダのHEMAや子供向けの商品に特化したアメリカのkidfreshなど、他とは違う選ばれた商品が並ぶスーパーが出現している。

本書では、まず最近注目を集めるトータルなブランディングを試みるスーパーマーケットを特集した。次に食品・飲料・生活用品のパッケージをカテゴリー別に紹介している。派手で目立つことよりも、ステイタスを感じるような洗練された作品が多く見られた食品。瑞々しさや爽快感の表現が様々で、見応えのある飲料。そしてインテリアとして飾りたくなるようなボディやバスケアの生活用品など、世界13か国のスーパーで販売されているパッケージを一同に集めた。

スタイリッシュでオリジナリティ豊かなパッケージは、消費者を惹き付ける要素を秘めている。毎日の暮らしに一番近いデザインだからこそ、美しくありたいものだ。

最後に、本書制作にあたり、素晴らしい作品をご提供下さったクリエイターの皆様、また快くご協力を賜った各社広報部門の方々に、心よりお礼申しあげたい。

ピエブックス編集部

Foreword

When I go overseas, supermarkets are one of my favorite places to visit. There you can see design that is embedded in the lifestyle of a place: the illustrations on dairy products, the packaging of sweets, items that have been around for years and the latest trends.

One advantage of the supermarket used to be that the products available were of the same quality whichever supermarket you visited, but now consumers who used to be satisfied with the same range of products are starting to favor supermarkets that have their own unique personality, that stock products you can't find anywhere else or design their own brand of products.

In the United Kingdom, your choice of supermarket is a reflection of your lifestyle. In San Francisco, supermarkets specializing in organic food have become hugely popular as part of the eco boom. From the Dutch supermarket chain HEMA that devotes time and effort to the design of its own products ranges and kidsfresh that specializes in products for children, we are beginning to see supermarkets that are stocking products that cannot be found elsewhere.

This book firstly features noteworthy examples of supermarkets that have undergone comprehensive branding, and goes on to introduce by category examples of packaging for food, drink and products for living. We have collected together examples of packaging used for products that are being sold in supermarkets around the world: food products where the packaging was largely high-end and refined rather than loud and showy; beverages with packaging that expressed the ideas of fresh and refreshing. Other products include body and skincare lines in packaging that that you could imagine as part of an interior decor.

The stylish and cleverly designed packaging contains numerous ideas for catching the eye of consumers. Because supermarket packaging is so much a part of our daily lives, we need it to be beautiful.

Finally, we would like to express our sincere appreciation to all the creators who took the time to provide magnificent examples of their work and the staff working in public relations divisions of various companies who cooperated in the production of this book.

PIE BOOKS

Editorial Note

Sainsbury's SO organic

Sainsbury's Organic Own-Label Range

セインズベリーオリジナル商品

CL : Sainsburu's
CD : Garrick Hamm
D : Grant Willtis
DF, S : Williams Murray Hamm

Supermarket PIE INTERNATIONAL **038** **FOOD** □Alcohol □Juice □Coffee □Tea

商品名またはブランド名 Product Name or Brand Name

商品の種類 Type of Work

制作スタッフ Production Staff

制作スタッフクレジットの制作者呼称は、下記のように省略して掲載しています。

The following abbreviations are used in for production staff names;

CL : Client	クライアント
CD : Creative Director	クリエイティブディレクター
AD : Art Director	アートディレクター
CW : Copywriter	コピーライター
D : Designer	デザイナー
I : Illustrator	イラストレーター
PH : Photographer	フォトグラファー
A : Agency	代理店
DF : Design Firm	制作会社
S : Submittor	作品提供者

上記以外の制作者呼称は、省略せずに記載しています。

Full name of all others involved in the creation / production of the work.

カテゴリー Category

SUPERMARKET BRANDING

CI・VIを始めパッケージなど、トータルなデザインを展開するスーパーマーケット特集。

A collection of noteworthy examples of supermarkets that have undergone comprehensive branding - from visual and corporate identity to packaging design.

HEMA / Waitrose / Berkeley Bowl Marketplace / Rainbow Grocery / Super de Boer / KINOKUNIYA / fresh & easy / kidfresh

SPECIAL 01

A design strategy that has captured many fans with an innovative rebranding of corporate and visual identity, from the Dutch company HEMA

革新的なCI・VIリニューアルで多くのファンを獲得したオランダ「HEMA」のデザイン戦略

Reporting / Text / Photographs (p.008, p.011) : ユイキヨミ Kiyomi Yui

HEMA

ヘマ

HEMA Amsterdam-Nieuwendijk
Nieuwendijk 174-176, 1012 MT Amsterdam
www.hema.nl

国内を中心に、約450店舗のチェーンを展開する大手スーパーマーケット「ヘマ」。1926年、アムステルダムに第1号店をオープンして以来「庶民の味方」として愛されてきたが、'80年代初頭からデザイン・コンシャスなブランドとしての方向性を打ち出し、ファン層をさらに拡張した。

最近では、商品や広告チャネルの多様化を受けて、パッケージ、CIやVIを次々とリニューアルして、国際的な脚光を浴びた。

この一連のデザインを手がけたのは、アムステルダムのデザイン事務所「クウェーデン・ポスツマ」(以下KP)。企業や省庁のCI、VIで数々の傑作を生み出す注目の事務所だ。

2003年、ヘマは大半の商品のパッケージをリニューアルするに当たって、「パッケージ・デザインは初めて」というKPを敢えて抜擢する。KPのクリエイティブ・ディレクタージャック・クウェーデンは、「国内では、5, 6社のデザイン事務所がパッケージに特化していて市場を独占している。ヘマは、他社製品と競う必要のない"モノ・ブランド"なので、マーケット・コードを巧みに使いこなすビジュアルではなく、革新的でダイレクトにコミュニケートするデザインを求めていた」と言う。

それらのパッケージの中でも、ひときわ注目を集めたのはハウス・ワインのラベル(P.014)だ。各ワインの味を、エレガントな植物写真で直感的に表現するという斬新な発想は、商品と消費者との間に新しい情報伝達の方法を築き上げたと絶賛された。

そして2007年、新CI、VIを発表。「ヘマのイメージは全国民に浸透している。だから問題点を解決しつつも、よい点はしっかりと残して更に強調することが、今回のリニューアルの目的だった」と、担当デザイナーのエディ・ウェグマンとメノー・ファン・ワーデハウゼンは語る。

ロゴは、赤の文字と青のアンダーラインという旧デザインから、正方形の色面にHEMAの文字を白抜きにしたスタンプ風にして、何色の地にも映えるように改善。だがタイプフェイスにはほとんど手をつけず、見慣れた4文字を強調するようデザインされた。

広告では、まるでトイカメラで撮影したようなライブ感溢れるスナップ写真が、厳密に作り込んだモデル写真に取って代わった。見る者に好感と親近感を与えるこれらの写真は、「日常」との関連性を強調し、ヘマのスタンスとビジョンをより明らかにしている。

さらに、「セール」「新作」など、情報の種類毎に色分けするというルールをつくり、煩雑になりやすい情報を整理した。その結果、店内のディスプレイにも統制が生まれている。

このように、情報をより直感的かつダイレクトな視覚言語に変換することによって、コミュニケーションのクオリティをも向上させるのが、KPのデザインの特徴だ。

ヘマのプロジェクトのメンバー。左からジャック・クウェーデン / エディ・ウェグマン / メノー・ファン・ワーデハウゼン。
The HEMA project team. From left, Jacques Koeweiden, Eddy Wegman and Menno van Waardhuizen.

Former Logo
旧ロゴ

New Logo
新ロゴ

カラーバリエーションが豊富な新ロゴ
New logo applied in a rich range of color variations

The major supermarket chain HEMA has approximately 450 stores, mainly in the Netherlands. Since its first store opened in Amsterdam in 1926, it has been considered "a friend of common people" and at the start of the 1980s established the direction of its design-conscious brand, thereby expanding its fan base.
In recent times, it has been placed in the international spotlight by successively rebranding its packaging and its corporate and visual identity.
The company responsible for these design projects was the Amsterdam design firm Koeweiden Postma (KP) who has gained a reputation for creating numerous masterpieces of corporate and visual identity for companies and government agencies.
In 2003, HEMA courageously selected KP, who had never previously designed packaging, for the rebranding of a substantial part of their packaging range. "In Holland there are five or six companies that specialize in packaging design and they dominate the market," says KP's director, Jacques Koeweiden. Because HEMA is a "mono-brand' that doesn't have to compete with competitors' products, HEMA was looking for an innovative design that communicated directly, not visuals that skilfully manipulated market codes."
Among the packaging, a label for a house wine attracted significant attention. The novel idea of intuitively expressing the flavor of each wine using photographs of elegant foliage was lauded for creating a new method of communication between the product and the consumer.
In 2007, the new corporate and visual identities were revealed. "The HEMA image is recognized by all Dutch people. The aim of this rebranding therefore was to resolve any problems at the same time as emphasizing the good things they had," say head designers Eddy Wegman and Menno van Waardhuizen.
From the former logo design with its red lettering and blue underline, the new logo was designed in the style of a stamp with the letters HEMA dropped out of a colored square, making the letters look good against a background of any color. The typeface was hardly changed at all and designed to emphasize the four familiar HEMA letterforms.
In the advertising, the carefully produced photographs of models were replaced with lively snapshots as if taken with a toy camera, snapshots that exuded a sense of "being live". These photographs that made the viewer feel good and imparted a sense of familiarity emphasized the connection with "daily life", making HEMA's stance and vision even clearer.
Rules were devised for color classification of different types of information, for example, "sale" or "new product", thus organizing information that was liable to become complicated. The in-store displays were also controlled as a result.
KP's design is about enhancing the quality of communication by converting information with a more intuitive and direct visual language in this way.

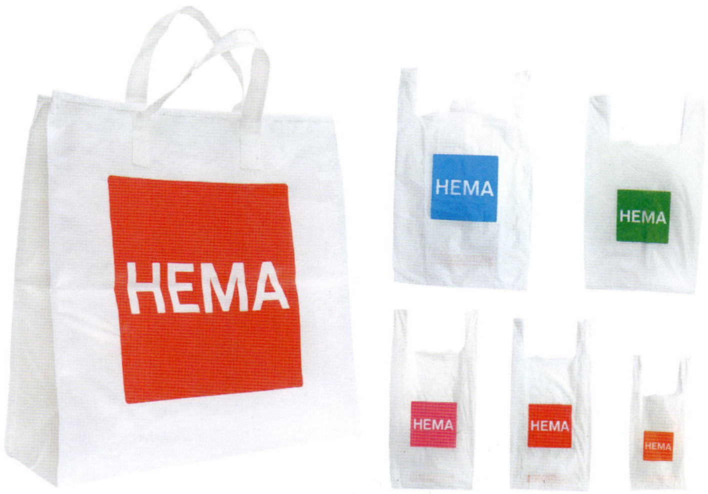

ロゴが映えるショッピングバッグ
The new logo reflected in a rich range of color variations

特価品、バーゲンのサイン
Icon used on packaging to signal special pricing

統制の取れたディスプレイ
The results controlled displays

ライブ感のある写真が生きるチラシ。
Leaflets feature photography that celebrates being alive.

左：「日常」を生き生きと描きだす写真が、見る者に親近感を与えるチラシ。
右ページ：色やフォルムに統制のあるサインやポスターは、店内に統一感を与える。
Left: Readers glean a sense of affinity from leaflet photos featuring people living everyday life with zest.
Right page: Color- and format-controlled signs and posters give store interiors a sense of unity. .

広告写真
Advertising photography

ook bij HEMA geldt per 1 juli 2008 een rookverbod
BUFFET
HEMA

HEMA
nu
nu
10.-
4.-

20% korting
SHAMPOO
CONDITIONER
alle shampoos en conditioners
Diverse soorten en verpakkingen.
20% korting

VISUAL IMAGE

デジタルな雰囲気から脱出し、食材のナチュラルさを表現するために、手描きのイラストを採用。色彩やラインを使って、多彩な表現を生み出している。
Hand-drawn illustrations were used as a way of avoiding a digital look and to express the naturalness of the ingredients. Varied expression was achieved using color and lines.

オイル＆ビネガー
Oil and Vinegar

デリカテッセンの各商品
Delicatessen Items

テイクアウトの商品には、スピード感のあるタイプフェイスを考案した。商品をイメージさせるカラーをラベルに付加しただけの、ミニマムながらもインパクトのあるラベル・デザイン。
The typeface featured on takeaway items was designed to impart a sense of speed. Labels are of a color commonly associated with the product making for minimalist, impactful design.

VISUAL IMAGE

各方面で絶賛されたワインラベルのデザイン。ドイツの写真家カール・ブロッスフェルド（1865～1932）のモノクロ植物写真を使い、各ワインの味の印象を表現している。

The design for a wine label that was highly acclaimed in various quarters. The flavor of each wine was expressed using black-and-white photographs of plants by the German photographer, Karl Blossfeldt (1865-1932).

左ページ右上は、コーヒー。ミルクやソフトドリンクは、認知度をあげるためにマーケット・コードを意識したラベル・デザインにした。
On the opposite page at the upper right is the coffee packaging. Milk and soft drink labels feature the market code prominently to improve product recognition.

VISUAL IMAGE

食材をグラフィックのエレメントにし、料理をする楽しみを表現。形の面白い食材を集め、スキャナーでテクスチャーを取り込み、モチーフを作成。商品に関連する食材を組み合わせてデザインしている。

Expressing the pleasure of cooking with cooking ingredients as an element of the graphics. The motif was created by scanning the texture of various interestingly shaped foods with a scanner. The design comes from the combining of the ingredients with the products.

VISUAL IMAGE

カメラレンズの絞りの形をモチーフにデザインを展開。
A design featuring a motif of the shape of the aperture of a camera lens.

PIE INTERNATIONAL Supermarket

SPECIAL 02 The simple, sophisticated design you would expect from a store that believes in its products.

品質に自信を持つ店ならではの シンプルで洗練されたデザイン

スーパーマーケットで最初にリサイクル袋「バッグ・フォー・ライフ」を導入したのがウェイトローズ。使えなくなったら新しいものと交換できる。1袋10Pで販売。
Waitrose was first to introduce the reusable 'bag for life', which they sell for 10p.

Waitrose
ウェイトローズ

Reporting / Text : 寺島彩子 Ayako Terashima
Photographs : 中臺隆平 Ryuhei Nakadai

The United Kingdom where a person's supermarket choice is also a lifestyle choice. In a country where the supermarket you frequent is an indication of your social class, Waitrose is known as a purveyor to the middle and upper classes. Its prices are set slightly higher than other supermarkets, but since it was established in the 1950s, it has persisted, in a tasteful manner, in providing the highest quality ingredients to its customers, by among other things supplying fresh locally sourced produce and supporting local farmers. Waitrose could even be described, not as a supermarket, but as a kind of department store that stocks selected specialty foods. The sophisticated packaging design and the beautifully maintained store displays have played a part in establishing Waitrose's inimitable brand image and the seemingly ordinary space we know as a supermarket makes customers feel good, serving as a way to a better life to which so many people aspire.

The three major basic tones of light honewort green, deep olive green and white were used for the logo, packaging and carrier bags and store signage to produce an elegant, composed environment. In contrast, the company's own "Waitrose" font used was inspired by the Gill and Futura fonts, and although traditional, has a pop look about it. It not only serves the basic purpose of being concise, but also demonstrates an ability to enhance the beauty of the design and the attractiveness of the products.

One further feature of the Waitrose packaging is the use of illustrations. In a world where it is taken for granted that photographs are used for product packaging, Waitrose breaks with tradition and used illustrations. Retro images are combined with a simple design to create delightful packaging design that almost make the products look like gifts. This can be achieved when you have confidence in your materials.

When asked what is the most important thing when it comes to Waitrose's visual design, the reply is "articulating the passion and the respect that Waitrose has for its products using a logical layout, persuasive images and skilled typography."

スーパーマーケットのチョイスはその人のライフスタイルそのもの、とも言われるイギリス。各ソーシャルクラスを識別できるスーパーマーケットが存在するなか、中流～上流階級御用達の店として知られるのがウェイトローズ。少々高めの値段設定だが、ギラギラした派手さはなく、1950年代の設立当初から、ローカルで取れる新鮮な素材の提供や農家のサポートなど、地道にクオリティの高い素材集めを徹底させてきた。スーパーというより、選りすぐりの専門食材を取り揃えたデパート的な存在と言えるかもしれない。さらに、洗練されたパッケージデザインや美しく整備されたディスプレイは、ウェイトローズの確固たるブランドイメージを確立させ、スーパーマーケットという一見普通な空間を、多くの人が憧れるような、より良い生活のコンシェルジュとして楽しませてくれる。

三つ葉の淡い緑とオリーブの深い緑、そして白という3つの基調色が、ロゴ、パッケージやキャリアバッグ、店舗の看板などに使用され、上品で落ち着きのある空間を演出している。一方、自社フォントの「Waitrose」は、「Gill」と「Futura」にインスパイアされたというだけあり、伝統的でありながら、ポップさも醸し出す。簡潔さという基本的な役割のみでなく、デザインとしての美しさと商品の魅力を引き立てる力強さも発揮する。

ウェイトローズのパッケージでもう一つ特徴的なのはイラストの使用だ。食品パッケージ＝写真というのが一般的な世界で、あえてイラストを積極的に使用。シンプルなデザインにレトロなイメージを加え、思わずお土産にしたくなるような可愛らしいパッケージデザインまでも揃える。素材に自信があるからこそなせる技と言える。

「論理的なレイアウト、説得力のある画像、熟練したタイポグラフィーにより、ウェイトローズが持つ良い素材への情熱と敬意を表現すること」それがウェイトローズのビジュアルデザインにおいて一番重要なポイントなのだ。

各店舗で配布されるフリーマガジン。季節ごとにおすすめ商品とレシピを紹介。
Their free magazine distributed in all their stores features seasonal products and recipes.

2009年春に発売された「エッセンシャル・ウェイトローズ」。生活に欠かせない良質な定番商品を手頃な価格で提供している。
In spring of 2009, the supermarket introduced its Essential Waitrose line of basic, everyday shopping items at affordable prices.

白を基調にし、可愛くさりげないイラストと文字は黒で統一。洗練されたデザインは思わずお土産にしたくなる。

The line's unified design features black type against a white background with sweet and simple illustrations and has a sense of refinement that almost makes the products look like gifts.

生スープシリーズ。具だくさんで素朴な味わいが伝わってくるような楽しいデザイン。
The canned soup series features delightful label design that communicates the hearty, rustic qualities of the product.

野菜ミックス、パースニップ、スパイシーポテトなど珍しい素材を使用したオリジナル・チップスシリーズ。レトロなイラストが普通のポテトチップスとは一味もふた味も違った雰囲気を出している。
Waitrose's original crisps series includes unusual items such as parsnips, spicy potatoes, and a vegetable mix. The retro-style illustrations impart a quality that sets them apart from typical potato crisps.

生産国の地図がパッケージに使用され、生産地が一目見てわかるチーズシリーズ。大胆なグラフィックのパッケージデザイン。
Packaged cheeses feature a map of the country of origin in a bold design that makes the source of the product clear at a glance.

PIE INTERNATIONAL Supermarket

SPECIAL 03 Health-oriented supermarkets in San Francisco and the Bay Area: friendly, representational design inspired by nature

自然にインスパイアされた、やさしく具象的なオーガニック系スーパーマーケットのデザイン ～サンフランシスコ&ベイエリア

Reporting / Text : 碓井美樹 Miki Usui (www.zakkanews.com)
Photographs : Lucy Goodhart

レジ脇で売られている、定番のリサイクルポリプロピレン製エコバッグ。マチが大きくとられていて、たっぷり入れられる。
Eco bag. Standard recycled polypropelene bags sold beside the checkout stations. With nice full gussets, one bag holds a heap of groceries.

CASE 1

Berkeley Bowl Marketplace

バークレー・ボウル・マーケットプレイス

2020 Oregon Street Berkeley, CA 94703
Tel +1-510-843-6929
www.berkeleybowl.com

大根を3本、地球を思わせる球体にアレンジして

バークレーにある巨大なスーパーマーケット「バークレー・ボウル・マーケットプレイス」。最初にオープンした場所が同名のボウリング場だったため、その名前を取って店名に。10年前に現在の場所に移転し、さらに売り場面積を広く、バージョンアップした。ストーンと開放感のある店内には、採れたての野菜や果物がアイテムごとに何種類も、市場さながらに並んでいる。サンフランシスコ＆ベイエリアのオーガニック系のスーパーではおなじみの、小麦粉やお米、ナッツ、ドライフルーツなどの量り売りコーナーも、かなりの充実ぶり。地元のものだけではなく、南米や、日本などアジアから直輸入したアメリカでは珍しい食材が揃っているのも、人気がある理由のひとつ。いつ訪れても、地元の買い物客で賑わっている。インパクトのあるロゴマークは、だいこんを3本、丸くデザインしたもの。30年前、日系二世の経営者が家族ぐるみで付き合いのあった著名な画家、小圃千浦氏の孫娘（当時、デザインの勉強をしていた）の作品だ。野菜や果物の種類の豊富さがこのスーパーマーケットの最大の特徴のため、野菜をデザインに取り入れてもらい、また、"日本の家紋のイメージで" とオーダーをしたのだそう。遠目に見ると、地球のようにも見えるこのロゴマーク。スタッフはもちろん、買い物客の間でも人気が高く、エコバッグやTシャツのほか、多くのオリジナル加工食品のパッケージに使われている。その際、周りを二重線で囲ったり、ロゴマークの下の地のデザインを変えたり、色使いも様々に。バリエーション豊かに、展開させている。

Three daikon radishes in a circular arrangement reminiscent of the earth

Berkeley Bowl Marketplace is a cavernous supermarket in Berkeley, California that first opened in a former bowling alley, from which it took its name. Ten years ago, the market relocated to its current premises, drastically expanding its retail floor space and ranking up its offerings and image. The Bowl's vast, open-feeling interior spills over with fruits and vegetables, with the multiple varieties of each item stacked in mountains reminiscent of a real farmers' market. Its substantial bulk foods corner – a familiar feature of health food-oriented markets in San Francisco and the Bay Area – sells lose grains, flours, dried fruits and nuts etc. Another feature contributing to the market's popularity is that in addition to its extensive range of the local items, it also stocks usual foodstuffs imported from South America, Japan and other parts of Asia. Hence the market buzzes with local shoppers at all hours of the day.

Berkeley Bowl Marketplace's striking logomark consists of three daikon radishes forming a circle. It was designed thirty years ago by famed Japanese painter Chiura Obata's granddaughter who was studying design at the time and was a family friend of the Bowl's second-generation Japanese owner. Because the market's pride was its abundant selection of produce, he asked her to incorporate vegetables into the design of something along the lines of a Japanese family crest. Viewed from a distance it also resembles the Earth. The logo appears on the Bowl's eco bags and T-shirts – popular with both staff and customers – as well as the packaging for the market's wide range of proprietary processed foods, where it is surrounded by a double line. The applications are in fact rich in variation, be it the coloration of the logo itself or the design of background it is set against.

デリコーナーで使われているプラスチック製の容器。ふたにロゴマークがプリントされている。ほかに、ガラスビン入り商品の紙ラベルやデリコーナーのプレートにもマークをアレンジ
Plastic containers. Also used at the deli counter. The logo is printed on the lids. The mark also appears on the labels of bottled items and plates used in the deli.

蜂の巣のハニカムをプリントしたラベルの上に、蜂蜜色のロゴマークをあしらっている蜂蜜。
Organic clover honey. Here a honey-colored logo is set against a honeycomb-patterned label.

左：鮮魚売り場に並ぶタルタルソース。マーブル模様の地にハンドプリントしたようなロゴマークが、素朴な雰囲気。中：ワサビパウダー。赤いキャップに合わせて、ロゴマークの大根の葉脈も赤い色に。遊びが効いた仕上がり。右：水分が多く甘みのあるGravensteinのリンゴを使ったソース。こちらもソースと同じ色のロゴデザイン。
Left: Gourmet tartar sauce. Sold at the seafood counter. The hand-printed-style logo set against a marble pattern creates a rustic look. Center: Wasabi powder. The veins of the daikon have been colored red to match the jar's red lid, in this playful rendition of the logo. Right: Organic Gravenstein applesauce. Juicy and sweet, Gravensteins are considered ideal for applesauce. Here too the logo has been colored to match the product.

オーガニックのブルーコーンで作られたトルティーヤチップス。深緑に白抜きのロゴデザインは目に鮮やか。
Blue tortilla chips. Tortilla chips made from organic blue corn. The white logo dropped out of a deep green ground dazzles the eye.

100%オーガニックのパスタ。ロゴマークは、パスタの色味に合わせてベージュとブラウンの色を使用。
Penne rigate. 100% organic pasta. Coordinated with the color of the pasta itself, the logo appears on the package in beige and brown.

左：店内のカフェでコーヒーを頼むとこのカップに入れてくれる。ふたがブラックになっていて、全体がひきしまったデザイン。右：生成りの紙袋に白地のロゴ入りステッカーがナチュラルなコーヒー豆のパッケージ。カフェインフリーのフレンチロースト。
Left: Paper cup. Coffee at the Berkeley Bowl Marketplace café is served in these cups. The lids are black which together with the cup create a clean, crisp look. Right: 100% Organic coffee beans. Unprinted paper bags with white stickers featuring the Bowl logo form natural-looking packages – here for the decaffeinated French Roast.

CASE 2

Rainbow Grocery

レインボウ・グロッサリー

1745 Folsom Street San Francisco,
CA 94103
Tel +1-415-863-0620
www.rainbowgrocery.org

スタッフのみに配られた、ロゴマークをあしらったマグネット。
Magnet. A flat sheet-type magnet featuring the logo, supplied to staff only.

太陽と虹と植物を組み合わせたナチュラルなデザイン

健康嗜好の人々、そしてベジタリアン（菜食主義者）、さらにはビーガン（菜食主義者よりもさらに厳格に、卵や乳製品も一切口にしない純菜食主義者）にも愛されているオーガニック系のスーパーマーケット。地元で採れたフレッシュな野菜や果物のほか、量り売りのナッツやチョコレート、パスタ、シリアル、コーヒー、お茶が通りに並ぶバルクコーナーは圧巻。豊富に揃う洗剤や化粧品、サプリメントも純粋な材料にこだわって作られたものばかり。販売している商品の約 90%がオーガニックだという。

30 年前にオープンした当時の初代ロゴマークは、英字の店名の上に、3 本線の虹を描いたシンプルなもの。現在のロゴマークは、14 年前に現住所に移転してから使用している 2 代目で、英字の店名を上下にあしらい、中央に、太陽と、4 本線の虹と植物をアレンジしている。このロゴマークをデザインしたのは、当時働いていた社員の友人のデザイナー。太陽と植物は自然の恵みを表し、店名でもある虹は、ベトナム反戦ムーブメントから端を発した 60 年代から 70 年代のヒッピー文化とも繋がる "自然回帰と精神主義" を象徴。このほか、"多様性" "共生" などの意味も込められている。これは、社員全員が株主の" A WORKER – OWNED COOPERATIVE" というスタイルの経営の考え方とも共通しているもの。

このロゴマークをあしらった商品は、エコバッグや巾着袋、アンブレラなど、数点。基本的には、グリーンカラーをメインに使っているが、虹を表すレインボウカラーでカラフルにロゴを彩った商品も見られる。

Nature-made design: the sun, a rainbow and flora

The Rainbow Grocery is an organically oriented supermarket loved by vegetarians, vegans and just plain health-conscious people alike. Along with the array of locally grown fresh fruits and vegetables, the aisles of bulk food bins containing everything from nuts and chocolates to pasta, cereals, coffee beans and loose tea are a sight to behold. Rainbow is rigorous about the purity of the ingredients in everything they sell from their wide selection of cleaning products to cosmetics and nutritional supplements. Roughly 90% of items sold in the store are said to be organic.

The Grocery originally opened 30 years ago with a logo consisting simply of a three-line rainbow set above the store name. The current, second-generation logomark – an arrangement composed of a sun, a four-line rainbow, and the branch of a vine bound top and bottom by the store name split into two lines – has been used since the coop relocated to its current premises 14 years ago, designed by the friend of a staff member at the time. The sun and the vine represent the blessings of nature, while the rainbow – also forming the store name – has its origins in the anti-Vietnam war movement and links to the hippie culture of the '60s and '70s as a symbol of "back to nature" and "spiritualism". Other concepts it embraces include "diversity" and "symbiosis", which relate to the business style of a worker-owned cooperative.

The logo features on a small line of proprietary items including eco and drawstring bags and an umbrella. It appears mainly in green, with a few chromatic applications in "rainbow" colors.

お店で使われている紙製のバッグ。店内にはリサイクルコーナーがあり、回収して再度使用している。
Paper bag. Provided for use inside the store. The bags are returned to the recycling corner in the store and reused.

左：人気がありすぐに売り切れてしまうという、オーガニックコットンを使った定番のエコバッグ。
右：ハンドメイドのオーガニックコットン製エコバッグ。ロゴマークを地色に合わせた色のグラデーションで表現。

Rainbow Bag Made of handwoven organic cotton fabric. The logomark is printed in a gradated tone to match the background color.

穀物や豆を入れるための袋。オーガニックコットンとパイル地の2種類、2サイズが揃う。

Drawstring bag. Bags for loose grains and beans. Available in organic cotton or terry cloth and in two sizes.

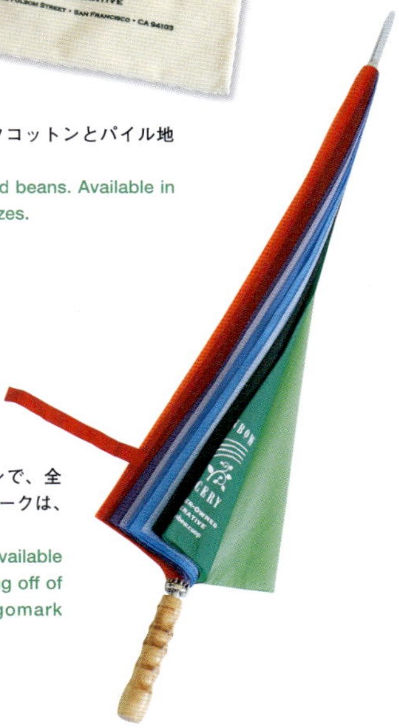

店名のレインボウカラーのグラデーションで、全16色が使われたアウトドア用の傘。ロゴマークは、緑色のスペースに白抜きデザインで。

Rainbow umbrella. An outdoor umbrella available in gradations of 16 rainbow colors, playing off of the coop's name. It all cases, the logomark appears in green and white.

SPECIAL 04 Changing from a 'me too' operation to a clear ownable identity

競合と差別化をはかる、オリジナリティのあるアイデンティティ

Super de Boer

CL : Super de Boer　D, DF, S : VBAT

ハーブティー
Herb Tea

牛乳
Milk

点心
Dim Sum

お米
Rice

サーモン
Salmon

ハーブ
Herbs

チョコスプレー
Chocolate Sprinkles

フルーツ風味シロップ
Fruit Flavoured Syrup

アイスクリーム
Ice Cream

SPECIAL 05 Packaging that boosts brand image in a trust-inspiring palette of greens

信頼感を与えるグリーンを基調に ブランドイメージを向上させるパッケージ

KINOKUNIYA 紀ノ国屋

CL：紀ノ国屋 KINOKUNIYA CO.,LTD.　AD：廣村正彰 Masaaki Hiromura　CW：三井 浩 Hiroshi Mitsui
D：中尾千絵 Chie Nakao　PH：近藤泰夫 Yasuo Kondo　DF, S：廣村デザイン事務所 Hiromura Design Office

ショッピングバッグ
Shopping Bag

パン袋
Bread Bag

パン
Bread

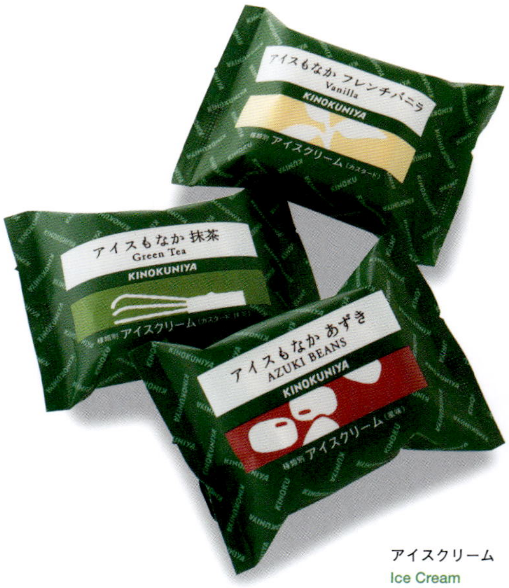

アイスクリーム
Ice Cream

アイスクリーム
Ice Cream

1

2

3

4

1. アイスキャンデー 2. カステラ 3. どらやき 4. 豆大福
1. Ice lolly 2. Castela 3. Dorayaki 4. Mame-daifuku

1

2

3

4

1. ごはん 2. 総菜 3. レトルトカレー 4. 調理済食品
1. Rice 2. Prepared Foods 3. Retort-pouch Curry 4. Prepared Food

SPECIAL 06 Wit and humour create brand character
知的で親しみの持てるユーモアで、ブランドの個性を作り出す

fresh & easy

CL : fresh & easy　CD : Simon Pemberton / Adrian Whitefoord　AD, CW, D : Lee Mewham / Phil Curl
CW, AD, D : Wes Anson　DF, S : Pemberton & Whitefoord

ユニフォーム
Uniform

ジャム
Preserves

トルティーヤ
Tortilla

コーヒー
Coffee

ポテトチップス
Potato Chips

SPECIAL 07

Cute, icon-like logo colored coded by ageat a supermarket specializing in products for children

年齢別に色わけしたキュートなロゴが目印の子供のためのスーパー

kidfresh

CL : Kid Fresh　CD : John Creson　D : Magdelena Hladka　DF, S : Addis Creson

牛乳
Milk

野菜ミックス
Vegetable medley

果物
Fruit

ショッピングバッグ
Shopping Bag

FOOD

Sainsbury's SO organic

Sainsbury's Organic Own-Label Range

セインズベリーオリジナル食品

CL : Sainsburu's
CD : Garrick Hamm
D : Grant Willtis
DF, S : Williams Murray Hamm

Fine cut
Seville orange
marmalade
6 apricot
cereal bars
...So you can enjoy a cereal bar that's Swiss and nutritious.
Made in Switzerland
where muesli was invented...
paghetti
Sainsbury's
SO
organic
Tuscan
bean
soup
Shortie
Biscuits
Horseradish
sauce
Italian
Extra virgin
olive oil
6 hazelnut
cereal bars
...So the hazelnuts feel at home...
Bran flakes
delicious whole grain wheat flakes
with added bran
500 gram
6 apricot
cereal bars
Cranberry
Juice drink
Chick
peas
in water
Sage and onion
stuffing mix
Oatflake & honey
cookies
Apricots
soft dried
ready to eat
Salsa
Raisins
washed and ready to use

Waitrose Original Foods

Sundaes サンデー

CL : Waitrose　CD : Perry Haydn Taylor　AD : Victoria Sawdon　CW : James Medd　D : Ruth Brooker　I, DF, S : Big Fish Design Ltd.　PH : Katie Hammond

Waitrose Original Foods

Frozen Desserts フローズンデザート

CL : Waitrose　CD : Perry Haydn Taylor　AD : Victoria Sawdon　CW : James Medd　D : Ruth Brooker　I, DF, S : Big Fish Design Ltd.　PH : Katie Hammond

Tims Dairy

Yoghurt ヨーグルト

CL : Tims Dairy
CD : Martin Dawe
AD, D, I : Angela Wilkinson
CW : Martin Brewer
PH : Tim Rose
DF, S : Martin Dawe Brand Design

Budgens Our Kitchen Range

Budgens Original Foods オリジナル食品

CL : Musgrave Budgens Londis
CD : Martin Dawe
AD, D, I : Steve Kane
CW : Isabel Goodman
PH : Tim Rose
DF, S : Martin Dawe Brand Design

Charlie Bighams

Prepared Food 調理済食品

CL : Bighams
CD : Perry Haydn Taylor
AD, D, PH, I, DF, S : Big Fish Design Ltd.

TESCO
Artichoke Hearts
in brine
TESCO
Leaf Spinach
in brine
TESCO
Whole Button Mushrooms
salt added
TESCO
Chopped Tomatoes
in rich tomato juice
TESCO
Fruit Cocktail
in fruit juice with vitamins A & C
TESCO
Italian Peeled Plum Tomatoes
in rich tomato juice
TESCO
Italian Chopped Tomatoes with Garlic
in rich tomato juice
TESCO
Italian Chopped Tomatoes with Garlic
in rich tomato juice
TESCO
Italian Chopped Tomatoes with Herbs
in rich tomato juice
TESCO
PARSNIP & BUTTERNUT SQUASH SOUP
TESCO
LENTIL & PANCETTA SOUP
TESCO
SWEET POTATO & CHILLI SOUP
TESCO
CHUNKY MINESTRONE Meal soup
TESCO
CHUNKY CHILLI Meal soup

TESCO Original Foods

Canned Fruit, Vegetables & Soup

フルーツ・野菜・スープの缶詰

CL : TESCO
CD : Dave Richmond
D : Iain Dobson
PH : Michael Michaels (Fruit & Vegetables)
James Murphy / Michael Michaels (Soup)
DF, S : R DESIGN

TESCO Original Foods

Pies & Quiches　パイ＆キッシュ

CL : TESCO
CD : Dave Richmond
D : Steve Sheffield / Sian Sargent / Jamie Lawrence
PH : Michael Michaels
DF, S : R DESIGN

dorset cereals Breakfast Cereal シリアル

CL : Dorset Cereals　CD, AD, CW : Perry Haydn Taylor　AD, DF, S : Big Fish Design Ltd.　D : Victoria Sawdon

Adamantina

Pasta パスタ

CL : Adamantina
CD : Yiannis Kouroudis
AD : Magda Theodoropoulou
S : K2DESIGN

FunWari Cake Dount

ふんわりケーキドーナツ
Donut ドーナツ

CL, S : Yamazaki Baking Co.,Ltd. 山崎製パン
2009年7月現在販売は終了しています。

KALDI COFFEE FARM カルディ コーヒーファーム Pasta Sauce パスタソース

CL, S : キャメル珈琲 Camel Coffee Co., Ltd. D : キャメル珈琲デザイン部 Camel Coffee Design Dpt.

HEMA Original Foods

Cereal シリアル

CL : HEMA
DF, S : PROUDdesign

SELFRIDGES & Co. Original Foods Grocery Range オリジナル食品

CL : SELFRIDGES & Co.　CD, D : Dave Richmond　DF, S : R DESIGN

SELFRIDGES&Co
FENNEL BISCUITS
SELFRIDGES&Co
MIXED HERB BISCUITS
SELFRIDGES&Co
DOUBLE CHOCOLATE CHIP BISCUITS
SELFRIDGES&Co
APPLE & CINNAMON BISCUITS
SELFRIDGES&Co
CHAMPAGNE BRUT
produce of France, MA-2851-20-00245, Élaboré à Pargny-Les-Reims par Médot et Cie à Reims, France.
SELFRIDGES&Co
CHARDONNAY VIN DE PAYS D'OC 2001
SELFRIDGES&Co
MERLOT VIN DE PAYS D'OC 2001
SELFRIDGES&Co
CHRISTMAS PUDDING WITH CHAMPAGNE
produce of England
SELFRIDGES&Co
HANDMADE PANETTONE

TESCO Original Foods

TESCO Value Range, Various Materials オリジナル食品Valueシリーズ

CL : TESCO
CD : Dave Richmond
D : Steve Sheffield
PH : Steve Payne
DF, S : R DESIGN

Halvors

Fish 魚

CL : Halvors
D : Sandro Kvernmo / Bjoern Viggo Ottem
S : Tank Design AS

Waitrose Delicatezze

Waitrose Original Foods オリジナル調理済食品

CL : Waitrose
CD : Julian Roberts
CW : Elise Valmorbida
D : Caroline Mee / Claire Hadley
I : Marion Deuchars
DF, S : Irving & Co.

Black Boy

Spices 調味料

CL : Rieber & Søn
CD : Morten Throndsen
DF, S : Strømme Throndsen Design

TESCO Original Foods

Herbs & Spices ハーブ＆スパイス

CL : TESCO
CD : Dave Richmond
D, I : Steve Sheffield
DF, S : R DESIGN

Black Boy

Spices 調味料

CL : Rieber & Søn
CD : Morten Throndsen
DF, S : Strømme Throndsen Design

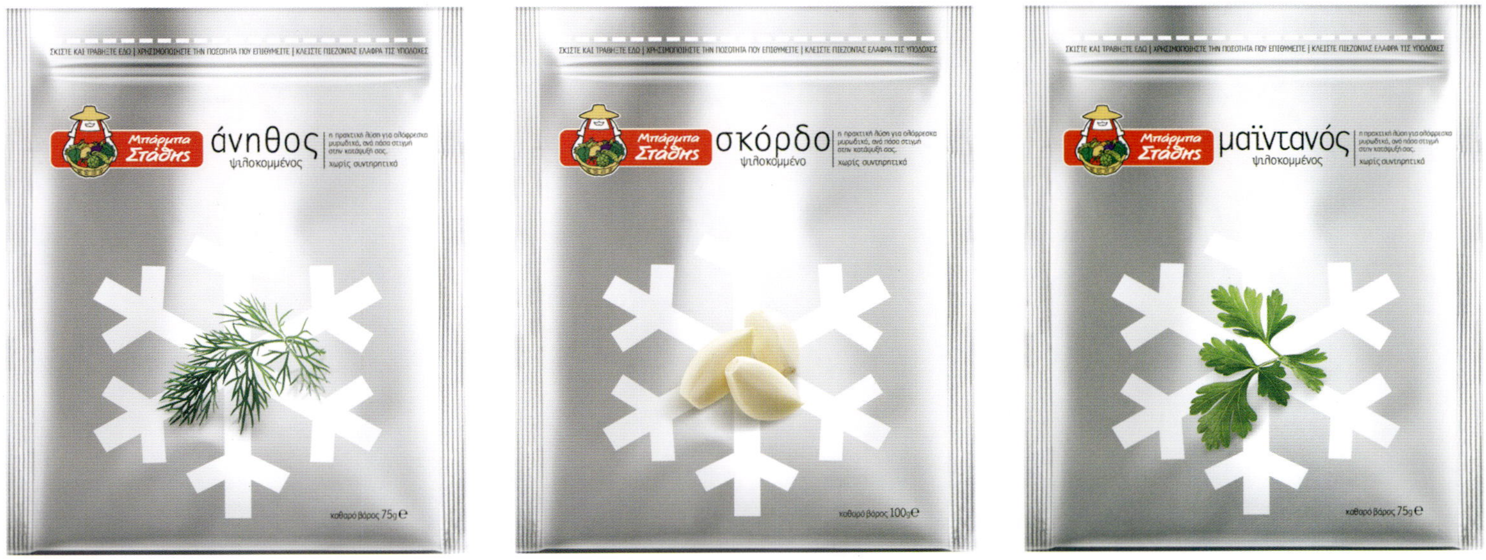

Uncle Stathis Frozen Herbs 冷凍ハーブ

CL : Vivartia Frozen Foods Division　CD, AD : Gregory Tsaknakis　PH : George Drakopoulos　I : Ioanna Papaioannou　Food Stylist : Tina Webb　DF, S : Mouse Graphics

Charlie Bighams

Prepared Food 調理済食品

CL : Bighams
CD : Perry Haydn Taylor
AD, CW, D, I, PH, DF, S : Big Fish Design Ltd.

Seven Cooker's

Sandwich サンドイッチ

CL : 7COOKERS SA
CD : Gregory Tsaknakis
AD : Alkistis Spilioti
PH : Tassos Vrettos
DF, S : Mouse Graphics

Whole Foods Market Original Foods

Bread パン

CL, CD : Whole Foods Market
CD : Patty Fair
D, I : Riley Hutchens
D, I, DF, S : Riley Designs

DEAN & DELUCA

ディーン＆デルーカ
Dipping Oil ディップ用オイル

S : DEAN & DELUCA JAPAN CO., LTD.

Hema Asia Series Original Food オリジナル食品

CL : HEMA DF, S : PROJDdesign

TESCO Ingredients Original Food オリジナル食品

CL : TESCO CD : Simon Pemberton AD, CW, D : Wes Anson PH : James Murphy DF, S : Pemberton & Whitefoord

La Belle Excuse Olive Oil, Vinegar, Vinaigrette オリーブオイル、ビネガー、ドレッシング

CL : Stavropoulos Olives Groves　CD, AD, D, A, DF, S : orangetango　PH : Marc Montplaisir

American Spoon Jam ジャム

CL : American Spoon Foods　CD, AD, D : Louise Fili　I : Charlotte Knox　DF, S : Louise Fili Ltd.

KOBERG VILT

Salami サラミ

CL : Koberg Vilt
CD, Project Manager : Ulf Berlin
Senior Designer, I : Cajsa Bratt
Production Manager : Louise Stierna
DF, S : Designkontoret Silver

CasCioppo bros.

Sausage ソーセージ

CL : Cascioppo bros.
CD : Steve Watson
D : Madeleine Eiche
DF, S : Turnstyle

Oshimugigohande

押し麦ごはんで

Prepared Food 調理済食品

CL, S : カゴメ KAGOME CO., LTD.
CD : 渡邉梨絵 Rie Watanabe (KAGOME)
AD, D : 牧野正樹 Masaki Makino (GK)
PH : 大手仁志 Hitoshi Ote (hue.inc)
DF : GKグラフィックス GK Graphics Inc.

Q.P. Hot Time

キユーピー ホッとタイム

Soup インスタントスープ

CL, S : キユーピー　Q.P. Corporation

DF : ライトパブリシティ　Light Publicity Co.,Ltd.

Japodon ジャポドン Retort-Pouch Food レトルト食品

CL : 大塚食品 Otsuka Foods Co., Ltd. CD : 能登健裕 Takehiro Noto AD : 橘野 準 Jun Kitsuno AD, D : 寒河江亘太 Kota Sagae PH : 大手仁志 Hitoshi Ote
A : 東急エージェンシー Tokyu Agency inc. Stylist : 渡辺美穂 Miho Watanabe DF, S : サガ SAGA inc.

Canyon Spice キャニオン スパイス Curry & Cream Stew Sauce カレールウ・クリームシチュールウ

CL, S : キャニオンスパイス Canyon Spice Corporation I : 大田原瑞穂 Mizuho Otahara

Ichido wa tabeteitadakitai Otsumami 一度は食べていただきたい おつまみ Side Dishes おつまみ

CL : なとり Natori　CD : 山本素久 Motohisa Yamamoto　AD : 矢口 洋 Hiroshi Yaguchi　PH : 鎌形貴司 Takashi Kamagata　D : 高濱 崇 Takashi Takahama　DF, S : デザインメイト Design Mate

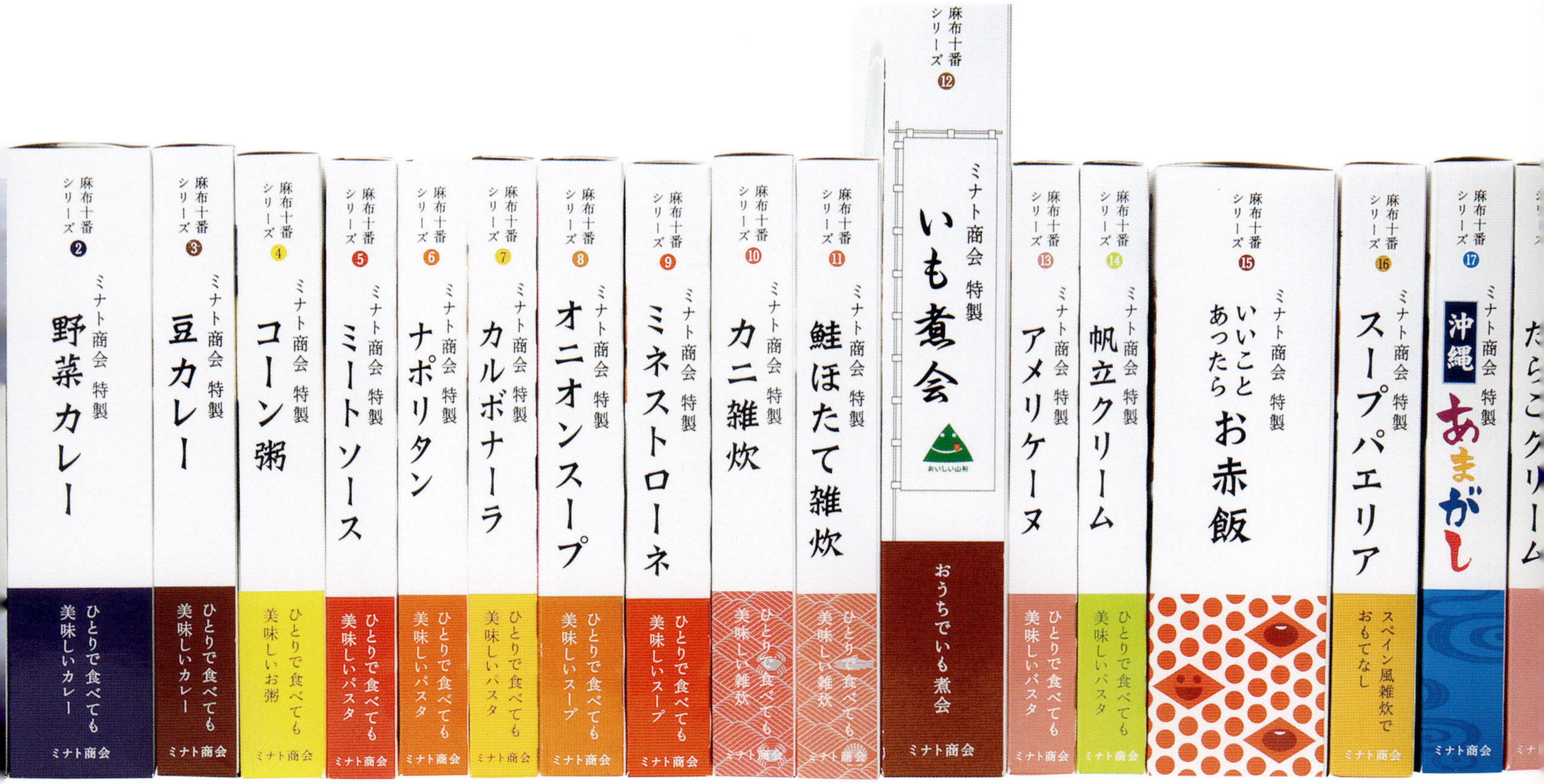

Azabu Juban Series 麻布十番シリーズ Prepared Food 調理済食品

CL, S : ミナト商会　Minato Shokai Co., Ltd.

Q.P. 3min.Cooking Yasaiwo tabeyo!

キユーピー3分クッキング 野菜をたべよう！

Soup スープ

CL, S : キユーピー Q.P. Corporation
DF : 山下デザインスタジオ Yamashita Design Studio

NISSIN Go Fan ニッシン ゴーハン

Prepared Food 調理済食品

CL, S：日清食品 NISSIN FOOD PRODUCTS CO.,LTD.
CD：小泉賢司 Kenji Koizumi
D：江崎涼子 Ryoko Ezaki
PH：飛知和正淳 Masayoshi Hichiwa
Supervisor：武田宣利 Nobutoshi Takeda / 金子大介 Daisuke Kaneko

Wakaori **和香り** Spice スパイス

CL, CD, S : ハウス食品 House Foods Corporation　AD : 桑 和美 Kazumi Kuwa　D : 高野樹子 Mikiko Takano　DF : プランタ PLANTA Ltd.

Tokachisan **十勝産** Tofu 豆腐

CL : 日向醗酵食品 HINATA HAKKO SYOKUHIN　CD, AD, S : ピーシーズデザイン pcs.design　D : 久保木明子 Akiko Kuboki / 重野真希 Maki Shigeno

Kanazawa Sweets 金澤スウィーツ

Pudding & Jerry プリン＆ゼリー

CL, S : オハラ Ohara Co., Ltd. D : 中田マコト Makoto Nakada DF : シュール Sur inc.

Naoeya Genbei 直江屋源兵衛

Dressing ドレッシング

CL : 直江屋源兵衛 Naoeya Genbei D : 橋本謙次郎 Kenjiro Hashimoto S : 直源醤油 Naogen Shoyu Co., Ltd.

One Dish Asia ワンディッシュアジア Instant Noodles インスタント麺類

CL, S : アライド コーポレーション Allied Corporation

Regioni D'Italia Pasta Sauce パスタソース

CL, S : 日欧商事 Japan Europe Trading Co., Ltd.

Green Curry & Red Curry グリーンカレー＆レッドカレー Retort-Pouch Curry レトルトカレー

CL, S : エム・シーシー食品 Mcc Foods Products Co., LTD　D : 木通いづみ Izumi Kidohshi　I : あくつじゅんこ Junko Akutsu　DF : アクアス Aquas

1

2

3

Saikyo 西京 1. Goma Miso 胡麻味噌 2. Sumiso 酢味噌 3. Dengaku Miso 田楽味噌 Miso 味噌

CL, S : 西京味噌 SAIKYO MISO CO., LTD.

Big Island Bees Honey はちみつ

CL : Big Island Bees　CD, AD, D : Louise Fili　DF, S : Louise Fili Ltd.

Favols ファヴォルス Confiture コンフィチュール

CL, S : ユウキ食品 YOUKI FOOD CO., LTD.

Renée Voltaire Eco Food エコ食品

CL : Renée Voltaire　CD, Project Manager : Ulf Berlin　Senior Designer : Eva Aggerborg　Production Manager : Caiza Nyman　DF, S : Designkontoret Silver

Premium Cornflakes プレミアムコーンフレーク Cornflakes コーンフレーク

CL, S : 日本食品製造 NIPPON FOOD MANUFACTURER　D, CW : 戸部 謙 ルイス Ken Luis Tobe

The Fine Cheese Co.

Crackers クラッカー

CL : The Fine Cheese Co.
CD, D : Julian Roberts
CW : Ann-Marie Dyas
I : Karen Murray
DF, S : Irving & Co.

Jordans

Cereal シリアル

CL : Jordans　Creative Partners : Karen Welman / Jonathan Ford　CW : Sylvie Saunders　D : Will Gladden　DF, S : Pearlfisher London

TESCO Original Foods
Doughnut & Cookie ドーナツ＆クッキー

CL : TESCO　CD : Spencer Buck　D : Karl Wills　DF, S : Taxi Studio

Zonnatura Kikker
Snack for Children 子供向けスナック

CL : Royal Wessanen / Zonnatura　D, DF, S : VBAT　I : Max Velthuis

Mondovino Savory Biscuits ビスケット

CL : Artisan Biscuits　CD, D, I : Julian Roberts　CW : Ann-Marie Dyas　D : Andrea Maloney　I : James Brown　DF, S : Irving & Co.

Two by Two Biscuits ビスケット

CL : Artisan Biscuits　CD, D : Julian Roberts　CW : Ann-Marie Dyas　D, I : Lucia Gaggiotti　DF, S : Irving & Co.

TESCO Original Foods Flour 小麦粉

CL : TESCO　CD : Simon Pemberton　AD, CW, D, I : Lee Newham　DF, S : Pemberton & Whitefoord

TESCO Original Foods Flour 小麦粉

CL : TESCO　CD : Spencer Buck　D : Karl Wills　I : Gary Bullock　DF, S : Taxi Studio

English Fruits for Cheese

Fruit Relish for Cheese 加工食品

CL : The Fine Cheese Co. CD, D, I : Julian Roberts CW : Ann-Marie Dyas DF, S : Irving & Co.

English Pickles for Cheese

Relish for Cheese 加工食品

CL : The Fine Cheese Co. CD, D : Julian Roberts CW : Ann-Marie Dyas I : Clare Melinsky DF, S : Irving & Co.

Kayak Ice Cream アイスクリーム

CL : Kayak　CD : Yiannis Kouroudis　AD : Margarita Nikitaki / Spyros Grammenos　DF, S : K2DESIGN

Little Dish Food for Children 子供向け食品

CL : Little Dish　Creative Partners : Karen Welman / Jonathan Ford　D : Claudio Vecchio　DF, S : Pearlfisher London

JME Snack スナック菓子

CL : JME　Creative Partners : Karen Welman / Jonathan Ford　AD : Natalle Chung　D : Sarah Pidgeon　I : Lucia Gaggiotti　DF, S : Pearlfisher London

Full Tank

Baby food ベビー食品

CL : Full Tank Foods
CD, D : Steve Watson
DF, S : Turnstyle

SESMARK

Crackers クラッカー

CL : PANOS Brands
CD : Stan Church
AD : Marco Escalante
D : Maritess Manaluz
I : Jeffrey Mangiat
DF,S : Wallace Church, Inc.

Pure Rich ピュアリッチ Yoghurt ヨーグルト

CL : チチヤス Chichiyasu Co.,Ltd. AD, D : 北川 正 Tadashi Kitagawa I : 加藤公太 Kota Kato Illustration Company : 象鯨美術 Zougei Art DF, S : 北川デザインオフィス Kitagawa Design Office

Ciao Bella Gelato ジェラート

CL : Ciao Bella Gelato Company　CD : Stan Church　D : Nin Glaister / Jhomy Irrazaba / Jodi Lubrich　DF, S : Wallace Church, Inc.

CONNOISSEUR Ice Cream アイスクリーム

CL : Fonterra Brand Australia Pty. Ltd.　CD, AD, D, DF, S : ASPREY CREATIVE　CW : Andrew Anastasious　PH : C.I.Studios

FRANGO Chocolate チョコレート

CL : Marshell Fields　CD, D, I : Scott Thares　CD : Richard Boynton　DF, S : Wink

Maui Chips マウイチップス Potato Chip ポテトチップ

CL, S : ソシオ工房　Studio Socio Inc　CD : 林 謙二 Kenji Hayashi　AD, D : 川島美智子 Michiko Kawashima
D : 山根彰子 Syouko Yamane　DF : アルスネットワーク arsnetwork

COOL Mint & Hot Cinnamon Candy キャンディ

CL : Red Dog Candy　D : Leif Steiner　DF, S : MOXIE SOZO

VITAMEAL Healthy Snacks ヘルシースナック

CL : VITAMEAL　CD, CW, D, PH, I : Irina Ivanova　DF, S : Irina Ivanova Design

TESCO Original Foods Tortilla Chips トルティーヤチップス

CL : TESCO　CD : Simon Pemberton　AD, D : Barry Crombie　PH : Laurie Evans　DF, S : Pemberton & Whitefoord

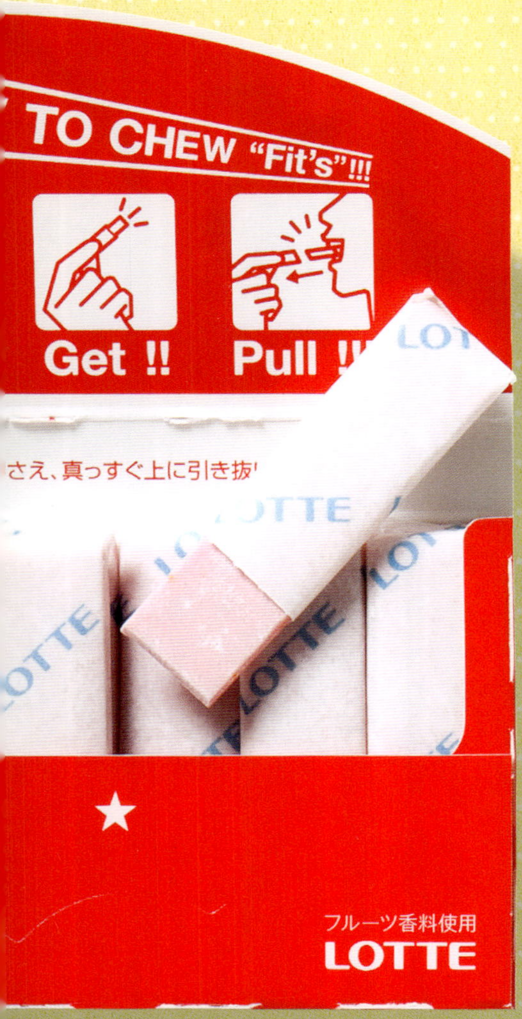

Fit's フィッツ Chewing Gum チューイングガム

CL, S : ロッテ LOTTE Co., LTD. CD : 和田 暢 Toru Wada AD, D : 土井宏明 Hiroaki Doi D : 五十川健一 Kenichi Isogawa I : 大野高史 Takashi Ohno
DF : ポジトロン Positron Design Co., Ltd.

PLUS X CUBE プラス エックス キューブ Chewing Gum チューイングガム

CL, S : ロッテ LOTTE Co.,LTD. CD : 簗 和夫 Kazuo Yana D, I : 宮 学 Manabu Miya DF : 共同印刷 Kyodo Printing Co., Ltd.

POs-Ca ポスカ

Chewing Gum チューイングガム

CL, S : 江崎グリコ Glico Foods Co.,Ltd.
CD : 江崎グリコ広告部 Ezaki Gurico Advertisement Division
Construction : 大日本印刷 Dai Nippon Printing Co., Ltd.

MEDISH メディッシュ

Chewing Gum チューイングガム

CL, S : ライオン LION Corporation
CD : 杉山 豊 Yutaka Sugiyama
AD : 調 進 Susumu Shirabe
CW : 吉岡丈晴 Takeharu Yoshioka
Producer : 新田大介 Daisuke Nitta
A : 博報堂 HAKUHODO INC.
DF : ライトパブリシティー Light Publicity Co., Ltd.

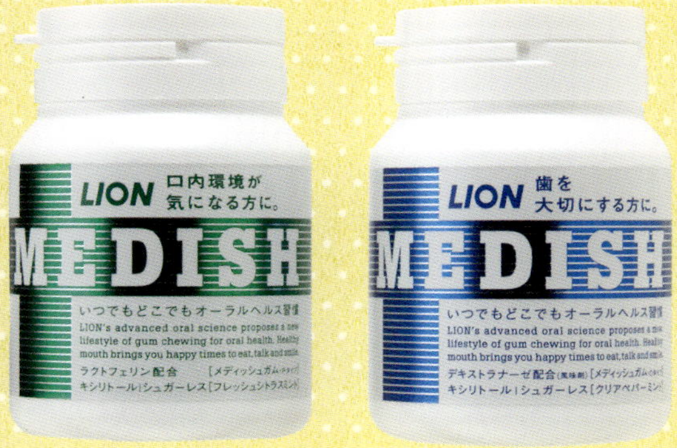

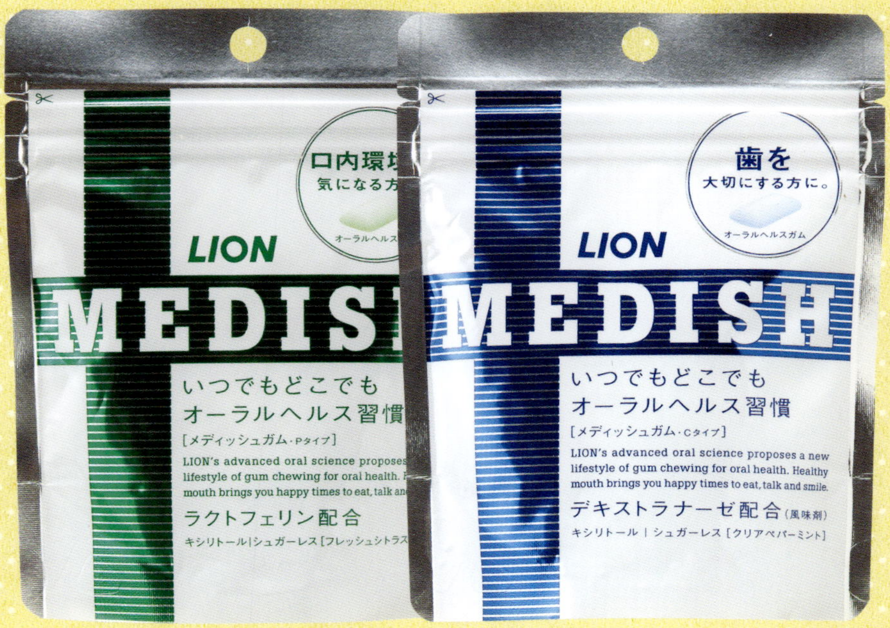

eco choco エコチョコ

Chocolate チョコレート

CL, S : ロッテ LOTTE Co.,LTD.
Producer : 白川義紀 Yoshiki Shirakawa
CW : 佐藤由起子 Yukiko Sato
D : 三橋美樹 Miki Mitsuhashi / 伊東美恵 Mie Ito / 新井美秀 Miho Arai / 飯沼規至子 Kishiko Iinuma / 三谷 健 Ken Mitani / 中尾英介 Eisuke Nakao
A : 電通 DENTSU Inc.
DF : たき工房 TAKI Corporation

Pharmaca Chocolate チョコレート

CL : Pharmaca Integrated Pharmacy CD : Pam Simich CW : Madeleine Berenson D, I : Riley Hutchens DF, S : Riley Designs

RICH Fran リッチフラン Snack スナック菓子

CL : 明治製菓 Meiji Seika Kaisha CD, AD : 菅原裕介 Yusuke Sugawara D : 矢口 洋 Hiroshi Yaguchi DF, S : デザインメイト Design Mate

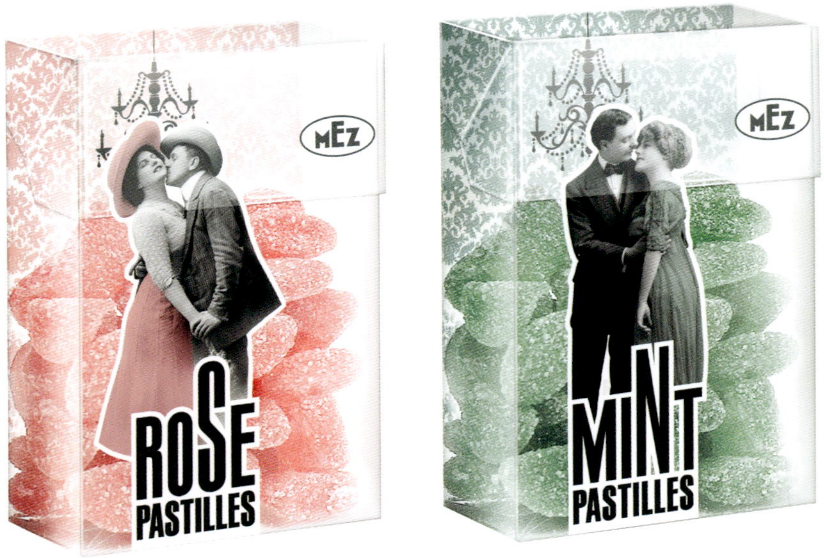

ROSE & MINT PASTILLES

Candy キャンディ

CL : Lavdas SA
CD : Gina Zafiraki
AD : Vassiliki Argyropoulou
I : Ioanna Papaioannou
DF, S : Mouse Graphics

SARADIS Lifedrops

Chewing Gum チューイングガム

CL : SARADIS SA
CD, AD : Gregory Tsaknakis
I : Ioanna Papaioannou
DF, S : Mouse Graphics

ICA Original Foods

Candy キャンディ

CL : ICA　CD, Project Manager : Ulf Berlin　Production Manager : Caiza Nyman　Senior Designer, I : Cajsa Bratt　DF, S : Designkontoret Silver

DRINK

Clipper Natural, Fair & Delicious Tea 紅茶

CL : Clipper Teas Ltd.　CD : Perry Haydn Taylor　AD, PH, DF, S : Big Fish Design Ltd.　CW : James Medd　D, I : Victoria Sawdon

NATURAL, FAIR & DELICIOUS
a delicious
tea anytime
80
BAGS OF OUR
FAIRTRADE
EVERYDAY
TEA
unbleached bags
250g
CLIPPER
NATURAL, FAIR & DELICIOUS
a delicious
tea anytime
40
BAGS OF OUR
ORGANIC
EVERYDAY
TEA
unbleached bags
125g

CLIPPER
NATURAL, FAIR & DELICIOUS
chamomile
20 BAGS OF OUR
ORGANIC
CALMING
INFUSION
unbleached bags
30g
CLIPPER
dandelion
20 BAGS OF OUR
ORGANIC
CLEANSING
INFUSION
unbleached bags
30g
20
BAGS OF
CLIPPER
NATURAL, FAIR & DELICIOUS
ORGANIC
DANDELION
INFUSION
30g
20
BAGS OF
CLIPPER
NATURAL, FAIR & DELICIOUS
ORGANIC
NETTLE &
PEPPERMINT
INFUSION
30g

pukka パッカ Herb Tea ハーブティー

CL, S : pukka Herbs Ltd (Import : 日仏貿易 Nichifutsu Boeki K.K.)　D : ニーナ・トムソン Nina Thomson / デヴィッド・トムソン David Thomson　DF : スペースクリエイティブ The Space

pukka
three mint
organic peppermint,
spearmint & fieldmint tea
to refresh & aid digestion

pukka
three mint

pukka
three berry
organic elderberry,
blueberry & blackberry tea
to nourish & restore

pukka
three berry

pukka

pukka
black
spiced chai
organic black tea with
cinnamon & cardamom
to warm & enrich

pukka
black
spiced chai

pukka
green
spiced chai
organic green tea with
star anise & cinnamon
to warm & enrich

pukka
green
spiced chai

pukka
three ginger
organic ginger, galangal
& golden turmeric tea
to uplift & warm

Moshi Moshi Mind Tea & Dietary Supplements 紅茶＆ダイエットサプリメント

CL : Moshi Moshi Mind CD, AD : Claus Due D : Henriette Kruse Jørgensen DF, S : Designbolaget

naturdiet

Dietary Products ダイエット飲料

CL : Naturapoteket
CD : Susanna Nygren Barkett
D : Johan Andersson
DF, S : BVD

Jaipur Avenue Chai Tea Mix チャイミックス

CL : Jaipur Avenue CD : Ben Graham D : Madeleine Eiche DF, S : Turnstyle

GRANOLA Coffee コーヒー

CL : Granola CD, AD, D : Claus Due D : Emil Gammelgaard I : Rasmus Meisler DF, S : Designbolaget

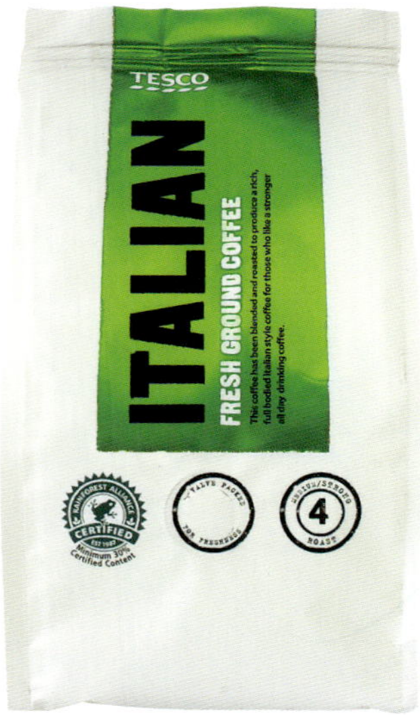

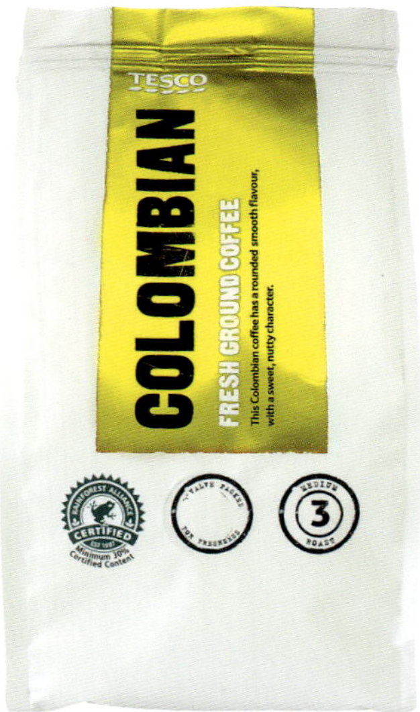

TESCO Original Products Coffee コーヒー

CL : TESCO　CD : Dave Richmond　D : Sian Sargent　DF, S : R DESIGN

JAVABICA Coffee コーヒー

CL, CW : JAVABICA　CD, D, AD, I : Natalie Wedeking　DF, S : WEDEKING / LAUN

Caffé Artigiano Coffee コーヒー

CL : Caffé Artigiano　CD, D : Roy White　CD, D, I, CW : Matthew Clark　DF, S : Subplot Design Inc.

HEMA Original Products Coffee コーヒー

CL : HEMA　DF, S : PROUDdesign

oops Wine ワイン

CL : Schwartz Ollcott　CD, AD : LiSA Simpson　Creative Partners : Karen Welman / Jonathan Ford　CW : LiSA Desforges　DF, S : Pearlfisher New York

Bartlett Wine ワイン

CL : Bartlett　CD, AD, D : Louise Fili　DF, S : Louise Fili Ltd.

Svedka Vodka ウォッカ

CL : Spirits Marque One　D : Sam O'Donahue / Stuart Devlin　DF, S : ESTABLISHED

Birds sing. Corks pop.
People laugh. Sounds good.
logan
Weemala
Brut NV

Weemala

Wine ワイン

CL : Logan Wines　DF, S : WAR DESIGN

Blossa

Liquor アルコール飲料

CL : Vas Group
CD : Catrin Vagnemark
AD : Susanna Nygren Barrett
D : Mia Heijkenskjöld / Sofia Ekwall
DF, S : BVD

Segredo
Alcohol アルコール飲料

CL : Athenian Breweries
D, DF, S : VBAT

Tiger Label
Beer ビール

CL : P&N Beverages　DF, S : WAR DESIGN

Iki Bottle 粋ボトル
Sake 日本酒

CL, S : ファミリーマート Family Mart
CD : 柳田美保 Miho Yanagida
DF : 柳田デザインスタジオ YANAGIDA DESIGN STUDIO

REFINED FLAVOR / LIGHTLY SWEET / ALL NATURAL / PURE CANE SUGAR
VARIETY 12 PACK: LAVENDER / JUNIPER BERRY / VANILLA BEAN // TWIST-OFF GLASS BOTTLES // 355 mL
DRY SODA CO.
v12
355 mL
DRY SODA CO.
VANILLA BEAN SODA
JUNIPER BERRY SODA
LAVENDER SODA
REFINED FLAVOR / LIGHTLY SWEET / ALL NATURAL
DRY Soda offers today's consumer the modern alternative in refreshment—a line of all natural, lightly sweet sodas, flavored with fruit, flower and herb extracts, and sweetened with a small amount of pure cane sugar. DRY's unique flavor profile and clean finish make it an ideal soda to pair with a great meal or a refreshing beverage on its own. For those who enjoy cocktails, DRY Soda also makes a distinct and sophisticated mixer.
www.drysoda.com
DRY PRODUCED BY:
SODA: VANILLA BEAN / 12 FL OZ (355 mL)
pure and aromatic. delicately sweet. all natural.
SODA: JUNIPER BERRY / 12 FL OZ (355 mL)
pine essence. crisp finish. all natural.
SODA: LAVENDER / 12 FL OZ (355 mL)

Dry Soda

Soda ソーダ

CL : Dry Soda
CD, D : Steve Watson
PH : Justin Gollmer
DF, S : Turnstyle

Tokachino とかち野 Wine ワイン

CL : 池田町ブドウ・ブドウ酒研究所 IKEDA BUDO・BUDOSYUKENKYUJYO CD, AD : 金澤和彦 Kazuhiko Kanazawa
D : 久保木明子 Akiko Kuboki / 重野真希 Maki Shigeno Fabric : 田中黎子 Reiko Tanaka
Logo Design : 桜陽 OUYO S : pcs. design ピーシーズデザイン

SAZAMEKI さざめき Alcohol アルコール飲料

CL, S : 白鶴酒造 Hakutsuru Sake Brewing Co.,Ltd.

Barokes バロークス Wine ワイン

CL, S : 日本酒類販売 Nihon Shurui Hanbai Co.,Ltd.

Nagomino Kajitsu なごみの果実 Alcohol アルコール飲料

CL : 菊水酒造 Kikusui Syuzo D : 吉村あずさ Azusa Yoshimura S : ナノ・クリエイティブ nano creative

Tottemo Tea とってもティー Tea 紅茶

CL：ネスレ日本 NESTLE JAPAN LTD. CD, AD：細島雄一 Yuichi Hosojima D：小林一彦 Kazuhiko Kobayashi I：マッシュルームカフェ mushroom cafe S：サンクディレクションズ CINQ DIRECTIONS

賞味期限
あけくち
Tottemo世界旅行!
NESTEA
Tottemo
Mango Tea
フルーティーなアップルマンゴー風味の紅茶です。
Mi Amigo!
Have a cheerful tea break with the fruity fragrance of mango.
期間限定
果汁1%
賞味期限
あけくち
Tottemo世界旅行!
NESTEA
Tottemo
Ichigo Tea
イチゴピューレで仕上げたコクのある紅茶です。
Ichigo Purée
Enjoy sweet tea with scent of strawberry. It's Russian tea time!
果汁1%
賞味期限
あけくち
Tottemo世界旅行!
NESTEA
Annin
Milk Tea
杏仁紅茶
賞味期限
あけくち
Tottemo世界旅行!
日本の春です。さくらミルクティー
NESTEA
Tottemo
Sakura
Milk Tea
さくらんぼと桜の香りの紅茶です。
Enjoy the new cherry-flavored milk tea and welcome the coming of spring.
果汁1%

NESTEA
Tottemo
Milk Tea
まろやか風味の
とっておきミルクティー
Enjoy the elegant and rich aroma of tea and creamy taste of milk which will bring you happiness.
280g
NESTEA
Tottemo
Milk Tea
500ml
Enjoy the elegant and rich aroma of tea and creamy taste of milk which will bring you happiness.
まろやか風味のとっておきミルクティー
NESTEA
Tottemo
Milk Tea
500ml
Enjoy the elegant and rich aroma of tea and creamy taste of milk which will bring you happiness.
まろやか風味のとっておきミルクティー
NESTEA
Tottemo
Milk Tea
500ml
Enjoy the elegant and rich aroma of tea and creamy taste of milk which will bring you happiness.
まろやか風味のとっておきミルクティー

ICA Original Products Yoghurt ヨーグルト

CL : ICA　CD, Project Manager : Ulf Berlin　D : Kina Giesenfeld-Herner　I : Kari Modén　Production Manager : Caiza Nyman　DF, S : Designkontoret Silver

Diet Rite

Juice ジュース

CL : P&N Beverages
DF, S : WAR DESIGN

ICA Original Products

Juice ジュース

CL : ICA
CD, Project Manager : Ulf Berlin
D : Linus Östberg
PH : Roland Persson
Production Manager : Caiza Nyman
DF, S : Designkontoret Silver

AB Vassilopoulos

Fresh Juice フレッシュジュース

CL : AB Vassilopoulos
CD : Gregory Tsaknakis
AD : Eva Bre
I : Ioanna Papaioannou
DF, S : Mouse Graphics

DR Stuarts Herbal Tea ハーブティ

CL : DR Stuarts　Creative Partners : Karen Welman / Jonathan Ford　CW : Lisa Desforges　D : Natalle Chung　I : Brett Ryder　DF, S : Pearlfisher London

Sunkist Fruit Juice フルーツジュース

CL : Sunkist　Creative Partners : Karen Welman / Jonathan Ford　D : Claudio Vecchld　DF, S : Pearlfisher London

this water

Fruit Juice フルーツジュース

CL : Innocent Drinks
Creative Partners : Karen Welman / Jonathan Ford
AD : Natalie Chung
D : Sarah Pidgeon
DF, S : Pearlfisher London

TESCO Original Products

Flavoured Milks フレーバーミルク

CL : TESCO
CD : Simon Pemberton
AD, D, I, CW : Lee Mewham
DF, S : Pemberton & Whitefoord

Happy Planet Shots

All-Natural Functional Shots ナチュラル栄養ドリンク

CL : Happy Planet Shots
CD, D : Roy White
CD, I : Matthew Clark
I : Steph Gibson
DF, S : Subplot Design Inc.

Le café ルカフェ

Tea 茶

CL, S : 茶香坊 Chakoubou

Human

Organic Super Juice

オーガニックジュース

CL : Kildespring A/S
CD : Jan Inge Bjöklund
PH : Anne Styrbech
DF, S : BJÖRKLUND emballage design

fuelosophy

Juice ジュース

CL : Pepsi Co
S : hatch design

Pocket Juicer Stand ポケットジューサースタンド Fruit Beverage フルーツ飲料

CL : ダイドードリンコ DyDo Drinco, Inc.　CD, AD : 細島雄一 Yuichi Hosojima　D : 益子佳奈 Kana Mashiko　I : マッシュルームカフェ mushroom cafe　S : サンクディレクションズ CINQ DIRECTIONS

ORGANIC MULLING SPICES

Mulling Spice ドリンク用スパイス

CL : Heron Valley Organic　CD, I : Blair Thomson　AD : BT Thomson　D : Bkar Thomson / Paul Warren
I : Stock Imagery　DF, S : biz-R

juice it up

Juice ジュース

CL : National Foods
CD : Peter Asprey
AD, D, I : George Margaritis
DF, S : ASPREY CREATIVE

inner ēco

Beverage 飲料

CL : Inner Eco
CD, D : Riley Hutchens
D, DF, S : Riley Designs

WB&CO VEG.JUICE Pure Organic Vegetable Juice オーガニック野菜ジュース

CL : WB&CO VEG.JUICE　CD, AD, D : Mark Walker　D : Mr. Garnet Teo　PH : Olivier Henry　A, DF, S : Seed Creative Consultants, Singapore

12 INCHES Beverage 飲料

CL : 12 INCHES　D : Ivana Martinovic　DF, S : WAR DESIGN

RIMI

Juice ジュース

CL : ICA (RIMI/NORWAY)
CD, Product Manager : Ulf Berlin
D : Kina Giesenfeld-herner
PH : Roland Persson
Production Manager : Caiza Nyman
DF, S : Designkontoret Silver

Rijp

Fresh Fruits Juice
フレッシュフルーツジュース

CL : Fruity King
CD : Bart de Rooy
D : Iwan Kempe
PH : Eric Zee Wilkin's
DF, S : PROUDdesign

Yasaishibori やさいしぼり

Vegetable Juice 野菜ジュース

CL, S, CD : カゴメ KAGOME CO., LTD.
CD : 博報堂ブランドデザイン HAKUHODO BRAND DESIGN
AD : 渡邉梨絵 Rie Watanabe / 佐藤益大 Masuhiro Sato
CW : 佐藤恵子 Keiko Sato
D : 庄司順一 Junichi Shoji / 常世田慎吾 Shingo Tokoyoda
PH : 亀井友吉 Yukichi Kamei
A : 博報堂 HAKUHODO INC.
DF : リュウズデザイン ryus' inc.

Frũla フルーラ

Soda ソーダ

CL, S : 友桝飲料 TOMOMASU DRINK Co.,LTD.
D : 八智代 Yachiyo
DF : ウイロー WILLOW

Belvoir Fruit Farm

Herb Drink ハーブドリンク

CL : Belvoir Fruit Farm
CD : Perry Haydn Taylor
AD, CW, PH, DF, S : Big Fish Design Ltd.
D, I : Victoria Sawdon

fluid

Beer ビール

CL : Mack Breweries
D : Bjoern Viggo Ottem /
Bernt Ottem /
Sandro Kvernmo
DF, S : TANK DESIGN AS

Herb Water
ハイビスカス
Herb Water
ミント
Herb Water
カモミール
Herb Water
ネトル
Herb
Herb Water

Metromint メトロミント

Mint Water ミントウォーター

CL : Jon Weber
D : Rio Miura
A, DF : Soma Beverage Company
S : 大塚製薬 Otsuka Pharmaceutical Co.,Ltd

Relax リラックス

Herb Tea 草本果茶

CL : 統一超商
President Chain Store Tokyo Marketing Corp.
CD : 菅原裕介 Yusuke Sugawara
AD : 矢口 洋 Hiroshi Yaguchi
D : 平林美穂 Miho Hirabayashi
S : デザインメイト Design Mate

70°NORTH

Water 水

CL : Alta Water Company
D : Jens K Styve / Bjoern Viggo Ottem
S : TANK DESIGN AS

Herb Water ハーブウォーター Herb Water ハーブウォーター

CL, S : ファインド・ニューズ FINDNEWS CO.,LTD.

fully loaded tea Tea 茶

CL : FullyLoadedTea CD, CW, D, I : Matthew Clark CD : Roy White PH : Raeff Miles and Stock Photography I : Steph Gibson / Roy White DF, S : Subplot Design Inc.

CRAFT BEER Beer ビール

CL : Okanagan Spring Brewery　CD, D, I : Matthew Clark　CD : Roy White　PH : Clinton Hussey　DF, S : Subplot Design Inc.

Innocent Drinks for children 子供向け飲料

CL : Innocent Kids Drinks　CD : Nick Darken　AD, CW : Aaron Hinchion　D : Joe Holt　I : Gamille Bozzini　DF, S : ALBION

Karel Capek カレルチャペック Tea 紅茶

CL, S : ドトールコーヒー Doutor Coffee Co., Ltd.　AD, I : 山田詩子（カレルチャペック）Utako Yamada (Karel Capek)
D : 浅野かおり（カレルチャペック）Kaori Asano (Karel Capek)

Café au Làit カフェオーレ Café au Làit カフェオーレ

CL : グリコ乳業 Glico Dairy Products Co., Ltd　CD : 松本 巌 Gan Matsumoto
AD, I : 寄藤文平 Bunpei Yorifuji　D : 鈴木千佳子 Chikako Suzuki　A : 電通 Dentsu Inc.
DF, S : 文平銀座 BUNPEI GINZA Ltd.

HOME
Hmm,
is that
everything?

Moisturize
BODY SOAP
peach
400mL / 14fl.oz
Enrich
BODY SOAP
gardenia
400mL / 14fl.oz
Soothe
BODY SOAP
clematis
400mL / 14fl.oz
Tone
BODY SOAP
honeysuckle
400mL / 14fl.oz

MANGO
HAND SOAP
AROMARISE
PEACH
HAND SOAP
AROMARISE
COCONUT
HAND SOAP
AROMARISE
MANGO
BODY CREAM
AROMARISE

Aura Scent Body Soap & Soap ボディソープ＆石鹸

CL, S : ペリカン石鹸　Pelicansoap Co., Ltd.

AROMARISE

Hand Soap, Body Cream & Soap ハンドソープ、ボディクリーム＆石鹸

CL, S : ペリカン石鹸　Pelicansoap Co., Ltd.

CUCINA

Soap, Hand Wash 石鹸＆ハンドソープ

CL : Fruits & Passion
CD, AD, D, PH, A, DF, S : orangetango

Kings & Queens

Showergels シャワージェル

CL : Kings & Queens
CD, I : Yiannins Kouroudis
AD : Dimitra Diamanti
DF, S : K2DESIGN

Finest Health & Beauty Range

Body Care ボディケア

CL : TESCO
CD, D : Dave Richmond
D : Sarah Bustin
DF, S : R DESIGN

Fruits & Passion Face Care フェイスケア

CL : Fruits & Passion
CD, AD, D, A, DF, S : orangetango
PH : Marc Montplaisir

Natural Hair ER Series ナチュラルヘア ERシリーズ Hair Care ヘアケア

CL, S：グレース Grace Corporation D：丹羽達雄 Tatsuo Niwa I：澤村厚夫 Atsuo Sawamura

Aroma Dew アロマデュウ Bath Essence & Body Soap バスエッセンス＆ボディソープ

CL, S：クロバーコーポレーション Clover Corporation D：三宅ゆかり Yukari Miyake DF：エムズクリエイション M's Creation

Body Therapy Spa
Skin Care スキンケア

CL : TESCO
CD : Dave Richmond
D : Sarah Bustin / Iain Dobson
DF, S : R DESIGN

SKIN BOOST
Skin Care スキンケア

CL : TESCO
CD : Dave Richmond
D : Sian Sargent
DF, S : R DESIGN

Oriflame

Skin Care スキンケア

CL : Oriflame
CD, Project Manager : André Hindersson
Senior Designer : Linus Östlund
PH : Björn Keller
Production Manager : Anna Harrysson
DF, S : Designkontoret Silver

ATTITUDE アティチュード

Household Cleaners 家庭用クリーナー

CL, S : スプリング・グローブ・クレセント Spring Grove Crescent Co.,Ltd.
D : ジアン・フランソワ・ベルニエ JEAN-FRANCOIS BERNIER

FIANCÉE フィアンセ

Fragrance フレグランス

CL, S : 井田ラボラトリーズ　IDA Laboratories Co.,Ltd.

Nail Enamel Remober ネイルエナメルリムーバー　Nail Remober 除光液

CL, S : サラダタウン　Salad Town Co.,Ltd

Body Soap ボディソープ

CL, S : サラダタウン　Salad Town Co.,Ltd　D : 高橋茉莉　Mari Takahashi

Daub & Bauble Soap 石鹸

CL : Good Well & Company　CD, D, I : Richard Boynton　CD : Scott Thares　DF, S : Wink

GATSBY Moving Rubber Series

ギャツビー ムービングラバー シリーズ

Hairstyling ヘアスタイリング

CL : マンダム　mandom corp.
CD : マンダム 第一商品開発部　mandom corp.
AD : 重田元恵　Motoe Shigeta
D, DF, S : エイブルデザイン企画　Able Design Planning Co.,Ltd.

GATSBY Hair Styling Series ギャツビー ヘアスタイリング シリーズ Hair Styling Gel ヘアスタイリングジェル

CL : マンダム mandom corp.　CD : マンダム 第一商品開発部 mandom corp.　AD : 重田元恵 Motoe Shigeta　D, DF, S : エイブルデザイン企画 Able Design Planning Co.,Ltd.

Liese
Clear Cube Wax

リーゼ クリアキューブ ワックス

Hair Styling Wax ヘアスタイリングワックス

CL, S : 花王 KAO Corporation

F/P HOMME Personal Care パーソナルケア

CL : Fruits & Passion CD, AD, D, PH, A, DF, S : orangetango

GATSBY Fragrance Deodorant Spray Series ギャツビー フレグランス デオドラント スプレー シリーズ Deodorant Spray デオドラントスプレー

CL : マンダム mandom corp. CD : マンダム 第一商品開発部 mandom corp. AD : 重田元恵 Motoe Shigeta D, DF, S : エイブルデザイン企画 Able Design Planning Co.,Ltd.

LÚCIDO Hair Styling Series ルシード ヘアスタイリング シリーズ Hair Styling ヘアスタイリング

CL : マンダム mandom corp. CD : マンダム 第一商品開発部 mandom corp. AD : 重田元恵 Motoe Shigeta D, DF, S : エイブルデザイン企画 Able Design Planning Co.,Ltd.

Neutral Baby

Baby Care ベビーケア

CL : Intec
CD : Bart de Rooy
D, I : Lieke Dirkx
DF, S : PROUDdesign

blow Hair Care ヘアケア

CL : Blow D, DF, S : ESTABLISHED

Natural Soap

ペリカン自然派石けん

Soap 石鹸

CL, S : ペリカン石鹸 Pelicansoap Co., Ltd.

Kitchen Cleaner キッチンクリーナー

CL, S : アイセン工業 AISEN INDUSTRIAL CO.,LTD. CD : ライフデザイン研究所 Life Design
D : 橋本晃子 Akiko Hashimoto

L-PACK plala

エルパック プララ

Portable Toothpaste and Toothbrush set

携帯用ハミガキ・ハブラシセット

CL, S : ライオン　LION Corporation
CD : 寺沢 勉　Tsutomu Terasawa
AD, D : 柴田幸子　Sachiko Shibata

nepi nepi ネピネピ

Tissue Paper, Toilet Paper

ティッシュペーパー、トイレットペーパー

CL, S : 王子ネピア　oji nepia co.,ltd.
CD : 佐藤 仁　Hitoshi Sato
AD : 弟子丸宏　Hiroshi Deshimaru
CW : 並河 進　Susumu Namikawa
D : 高松法弘　Norihiro Takamatsu
A : 電通　DENTSU INC.
DF : ジェイツ・コンプレックス　j2 COMPLEX INC.

art home Cleansing Spray & Cleansing Hand Gel クレンジング スプレー＆クレンジング ハンドジェル

CL : Fruits & Passion CD, AD, D, PH, A, DF, S : orangetango

Maq Auto Washing Powder 洗濯洗剤

CL : Bliss Chemicals Ltd.　CD, D : Annie Moag　D : Kim Ford　DF, S : Moag Bailie

TESCO Original Products Cleaning Products クリーニング洗剤

CL : TESCO　CD : Simon Pemberton　AD, D, I, CW : Wes Anson　DF, S : Pemberton & Whitefoord

Better Life

Household Cleaners 家庭用クリーナー

CL, S : Better Life
CD, AD, D, I : Jen Halski
CW : Marc Chechik
PH : Geoff Cardin
DF : Halski Studio

TESCO Original Products

Household Cleaners 家庭用クリーナー

CL : TESCO　CD : Dave Richmond　D : Iain Dobson　DF, S : R DESIGN

Method
Air Freshener エアフレッシュナー

CL, S : Method Products
Industrial Design CD : Joshua Handy
Brand CD : Nate Pence
AD : Stephanie Hermsdorf
D : Danny Alexanoer
DF : Method in house

Method
Air Freshener エアフレッシュナー

CL, S : Method Products
CD : Eric Ryan
AD : Stephanie Hermsdorf
D : Karim Rashid Studio
DF : Method in house

Method Air Freshener エアフレッシュナー

CL, S : Method Products　Industrial Design CD : Joshua Handy　Brand CD : Nate Pence　AD : Stefanie Hermsdorf　D : Josh Handy

LE SCRUB

Bathroom Cleaner バスクリーナー

CL, S : Method
Brand CD : Nate Pence
Industrial Design CD : Joshua Handy
AD : Sally Clarke
CW : Mellisa Sheehan
D : Danny Alexander
DF : Method in House

LIL' BOWL BLU

Toilet Cleaner トイレクリーナー

CL, S : Method
Brand CD : Nate Pence
Industrial Design CD : Joshua Handy
AD : Sally Clarke
CW : Mellisa Sheehan
D : Danny Alexander
DF : Method in House

Method

Handwash ハンドウォッシュ

CL, S : Method Products
CD : Eric Ryan
AD : Stefanie Hermsdorf
D : Karim Rashid Studio
DF, S : Method in house

Method

Dish Soap ディッシュソープ

CL, S : Method Products
Industrial Design CD : Joshua Hanoy
Brand CD : Nate Pence
AD : Sally clarke
CW : Mellisa Sheehan
D : Joshua Handy
DF : Method in house

Relish レリッシュ Tights & Spats ストッキング&スパッツ

CL : アツギ ATSUGI Co.,Ltd. AD, D : 辻 直樹 Naoki Tsuji PH : 赤尾昌則 Masanori Akao (Switch) DF, S : 辻 直樹デザイン室 Tsuji Design Office

Walk Socks

Socks ソックス

CL : Walk Socks
CD, AD : Gregory Tsaknakis
DF, S : Mouse Graphics

MiawMiaw ミャウミャウ Cat Food キャットフード

CL, S : アイシア AIXIA CORPORATION A : 東急エージェンシー Tokyu Agency Inc.

Lily's Kitchen Dog Food ドッグフード

CL : Lily's Kitchen CD : Nick Oarken AD, CW : Aaron Hinchion CW : Natalie Ranger D : Joe Holt I : Petra Borner Producer : Ene Price DF, S : ALBION

INDEX

Client

Submitter

@Supermarket: Package Design
スーパーマーケットデザイン

2009年7月27日　初版第1刷発行

Jacket Illustrator
せき なつこ Natsko Seki / Taiko & Associates

Art Director & Designer
松村大輔 Daisuke Matsumura

Photographer
藤本邦治 Kuniharu Fujimoto

International Coordinator
岸田麻矢 Maya Kishida

Translator
パメラ・ミキ Pamela Miki

Editor
高橋かおる Kaoru Takahashi
数野由香子 Yukako Kazuno

発行元　パイ インターナショナル
〒114-0024　東京都北区西ヶ原4-3-6（東京支社）
TEL：03-3944-3981　FAX：03-5395-4830
sales@pie-intl.com
埼玉県蕨市北町1-19-21-301（本社）

印刷・製本　図書印刷株式会社

ISBN978-4-7562-4002-6 C3070
Printed in Japan

本書の収録内容の無断転載・複写・引用等は禁じます。
ご注文、乱丁・落丁本の交換等に関するお問い合わせは、小社東京支社までご連絡ください。